Most children go to school.

Travelling to school

Long ago children walked to school.

Then and Now

Life at School

Vicki Yates

www.heinemann.co.uk/library
Visit our website to find out more information about Heinemann Library books.

To order:
☎ Phone 44 (0) 1865 888066
🖹 Send a fax to 44 (0) 1865 314091
💻 Visit the Heinemann Bookshop at www.heinemann.co.uk/library to browse our catalogue and order online.

First published in Great Britain by Heinemann Library, Halley Court, Jordan Hill, Oxford OX2 8EJ, part of Pearson Education. Heinemann is a registered trademark of Pearson Education Ltd.

Editorial: Charlotte Guillain and Vicki Yates
Design: Victoria Bevan, Joanna Hinton-Malivoire and Q2A solutions
Picture research: Ruth Blair and Q2A solutions
Production: Duncan Gilbert

Printed and bound in China by South China Printing Co. Ltd.

ISBN 978 0 431 191881 (Hardback)

ISBN 978 0431 19196 6 (Paperback)
13 12 11 10 09
10 9 8 7 6 5 4 3 2 1

British Library Cataloguing in Publication Data
Yates, Vicki. Life at school. - (Then and now)
1. School children - Juvenile literature 2. School environment - Juvenile literature 3. School children - History - Juvenile literature 4. School environment - History - Juvenile literature
370
A full catalogue record for this book is available from the British Library.

Acknowledgements
The publishers would like to thank the following for permission to reproduce photographs:
Alamy pp. **14**, **23** (D. Hurst), **17** (Sally and Richard Greenhill), **20** (Popperfoto); Bonniej p.**11** (Dreamstime.com); Corbis pp. **6** (H. Armstrong Roberts), **9** (Will & Deni McIntyre), **22** (Bettmann); Flickr p. **19** (Glenn Loos-Austin); Getty Images pp. **4**, **15** (Photodisc); Greater Manchester County Record Office p. **10**, **18**; Library of Congress p. **8**; New York Picture Library p. **16**; Ottmar Bierwagen p. **7** (photographersdirect.com); Photolibrary.com pp. **5** (Photo Researchers, Inc), **12** (Nonstock Inc), **13** (Index Stock Imagery); SuperStock p. **21**

Cover photograph of slate reproduced with permission of Corbis (Tetra Images) and photograph of computer reproduced with permission of Alamy/archivberlin Fotoagentur GmbH. Back cover photograph of slate reproduced with permission of Alamy (D. Hurst).

Every effort has been made to contact copyright holders of any material reproduced in this book. Any omissions will be rectified in subsequent printings if notice is given to the publishers.

Contents

What is school?

School is where we go to learn.

Today many children go to school
by bus or car. Some children walk.

In and around school

Long ago schools were small.

Today many schools are big.

Long ago classrooms were cold and dark.

Today classrooms are warm
and light.

Learning

Long ago children learned a few subjects at school.

Today we learn many subjects at school.

Long ago children wrote on slate boards.

Today we can write with
computers.

Long ago schools had few books.

Today schools can have lots
of books.

Long ago children did PE.

Today children still do PE.

Let's compare

Long ago school was very different.

Which is better? Then or now?

What is it?

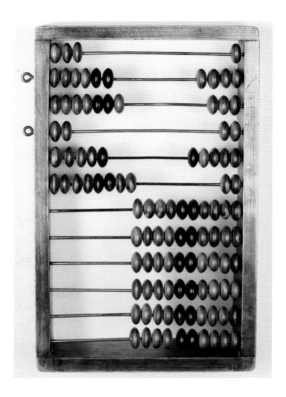

Long ago this object was used in schools. Do you know what it is?

Answer on p. 24

Picture glossary

slate board board made from a flat rock called slate. People wrote on it with chalk.

Index

Answer to question on p. 22: It is an abacus. Children used it to help them add up.

To Parents and Teachers

Before reading

Ask the children why they come to school. Write their ideas on a sheet of paper and display for parents to see. Ask them what they like doing best at school and tally the answers to find out what is the most popular subject or activity. Explain that schools have changed since you went to school. Encourage them to ask you questions about your school days.

After reading

• Play "When am I?". Explain to the children that you are going to describe something done in the school. They must tell you whether it is today or long ago. For example, "I am sitting at my desk."

• Using the tune and rhythm of "Early in the morning, down at the station", change the words to "Early in the morning, when we get to school/See all the children sitting in a row/See the tall teacher writing on the black board/Oh dear, oh dear, that was long ago." Ask the children to help you to make up some other verses about schools today. Write out the verses and record the children singing.